GEOGRAPHY ENCYCLOPEDIA

EXPLORING LIFE

Om Books International

CONTENTS

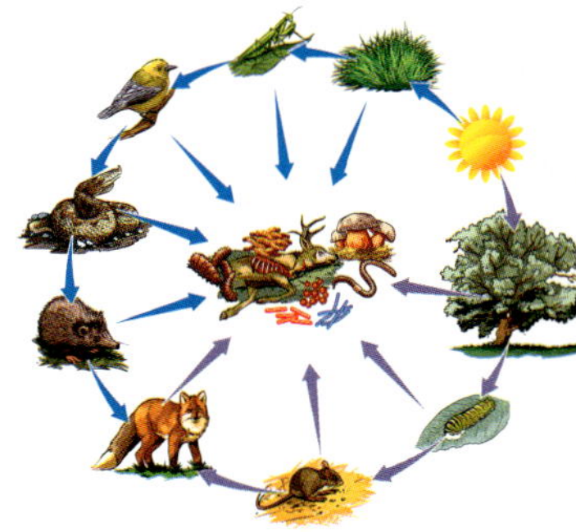

EXPLORING LIFE

Earth is distinguished from all other planets because it is on Earth that life exists. There is life on land, in water and in air. There are living micro organisms in the atmosphere, large mammals, various fishes and aquatic plants in the hydrosphere as well as humans, animals and terrestrial plants on the lithosphere.

As Earth is spherical in shape, just like the lithosphere, atmosphere and hydrosphere, the "biosphere" is described in terms of a "sphere". Eduard Suess, a geologist, first used this term in 1875 to mean "the place on Earth which contains life". It overlaps the study of all other spheres as it speaks of life and the waste products created by it.

ORIGINS OF LIFE

Before life came into existence, Earth's landscape was rocky and volatile. The seas were shallow and lacking in rich minerals. The air contained carbon dioxide, nitrogen, water vapour, hydrogen sulphide and carbon monoxide. Like the other planets, Earth was barren and inhospitable. However, with their interactions, the biosphere soon came into existence.

Ancient prokaryotes

The origin of the biosphere can be traced 3.5 billion years in the past when the first organisms came to life. The first living organisms were called "prokaryote", a term which is still used today to describe an organism that does not contain a nucleus in its cell. The "ancient prokaryotes", as they are called today, were single-celled organisms. It is assumed that these organisms could live without oxygen as at the time, oxygen was not present in Earth's atmosphere.

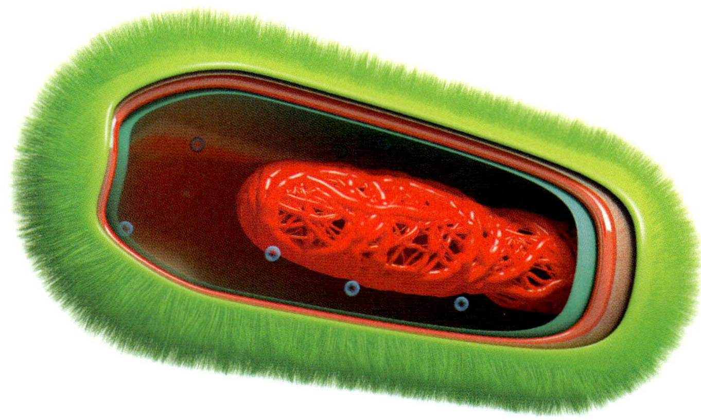

Bacteria is a developed and modern prokaryotic cell.

Developing photosynthesis

As time moved on, the relentless energy from the Sun resulted in the development of ancient prokaryotes. They were able to carry out the chemical process of photosynthesis to make water, oxygen, carbon dioxide and simplified forms of sugars in the presence of sunlight. They began to multiply, until there were enough prokaryotes to bring about the first change in the biosphere.

Complex life-forms

With the process of photosynthesis, ancient prokaryotes released enough oxygen into the atmosphere to change the gases present. The atmosphere then contained oxygen and other gases which could support life. This in turn helped develop organisms with complex structures. Soon, plants and animals began to cover Earth's surface.

The food web

Single-celled and multi-celled organisms such as bacteria and archaea evolved from this phase. These organisms, along with plants and animals, evolved to decompose and also carry out the process of decomposition. This brought on the development of the food web.

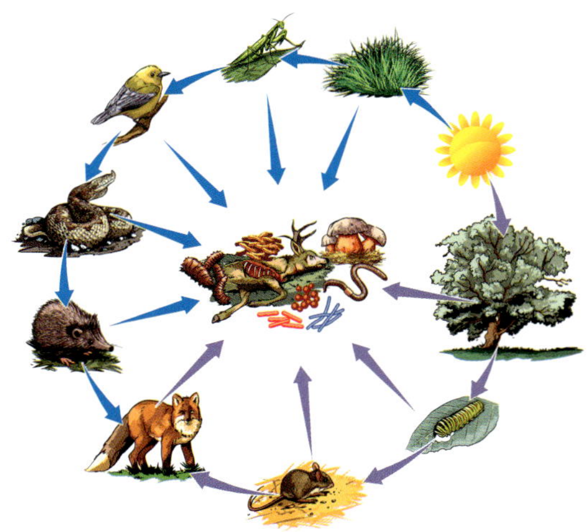

A diagram showing an example of the food web with present-day animals.

The earliest food web was quite simple. Dead animals and plants decomposed to release nutrients into the soil or water in which they lived. These nutrients were taken in by living and growing organisms. As a result, the biosphere became a system in which organisms supported and controlled each other through the course of their lives.

BUILDING BLOCKS OF LIFE

Biosphere is a thin layer of Earth's surface where life exists. It is the part of Earth which absorbs solar energy and matter to produce life. It extends from heights of about 10 km into the atmosphere to the depths of the ocean. It consists of all living organisms (biotic) and non-living factors (abiotic) from which the living get their nutrients and energy.

Building blocks of life

Of the different elements found naturally on Earth, around 11 are found in larger than trace (.01% or less) quantities in living things. The main elements are carbon, hydrogen, oxygen, nitrogen, sulphur and phosphorous. These combine to form carbohydrates, proteins, lipids and nucleic acids, the building blocks of life.

Carbon

The molecules that form life are mainly created from carbon. This carbon then combines with organic matter to produce proteins, carbohydrates, fats and other nutrients. Have you heard the term "DNA"? It is short for "deoxyribonucleic acid", which is received from the parent organism.

It is with the help of this DNA that living beings are able to self-produce proteins. The earliest DNA is said to have formed from chemical reactions that started as the result of electric energy from lightning.

Bacteria is a developed and modern prokaryotic cell.

Reproducing DNA

DNA is a molecule that allows a cell to reproduce by splitting into two halves. The lacking chemicals are added to both halves so that they can form more molecules and help produce proteins. The evolution of life took off with the development of the first cell.

Cell

Bacterium is the earliest cell that contained DNA along with water, nutrients and organic molecules. They were simple cells that developed into more advanced cells. This took place nearly 2.5 billion years ago.

These advanced cells had nucleus. DNA was contained within this nucleus. It had a complex structure in which different parts were used for different tasks. They were called "eukaryotic cells" and could convert food into energy.

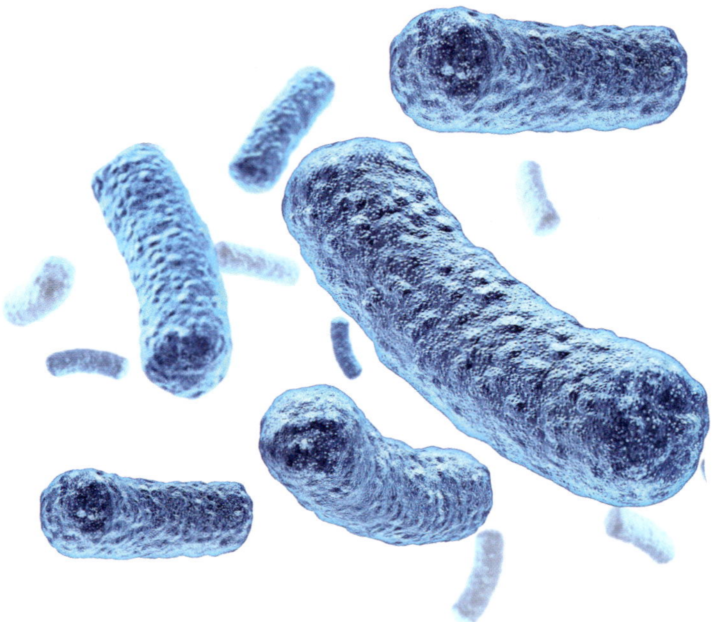

EARLY ORGANISMS

As the eukaryotic cell developed, each cell was able to specialise in certain tasks such as communication to different cells. Soon, many eukaryotic cells came together to form multicellular organisms such as the ancient Volvox, which was an aquatic organism.

Soft-bodied creatures

The earliest multicellular organisms had soft bodies and lived in the sea. Most of them slowly began to resemble the modern-day jellyfish. These multicellular organisms sprouted special and complex structures in which different cells or groups of cells performed tasks. The soft-bodied creatures were made up of more than one lakh eukaryotic cells. Some of them had parts resembling tentacles and reproductive organs.

Hard-bodied animals

Hard-bodied animals appeared on Earth nearly 500 million years ago. These animals had skeletons. Their bodies were made hard and strong by the presence of vertebrae. They were the earliest vertebrates on Earth.

Coelacanth

Coelacanth is a type of fish that is found in the waters surrounding Africa. It is called a "living fossil" as it was believed to gone extinct nearly 65 million years ago. However, the coelacanth still lives today. It resembles the earliest vertebrates, which came into existence nearly 100 million years ago.

An example of the Coelacanth.

Amphibians

The first amphibians are said to have developed from the fish that resemble the coelacanth of today. They are the ancestors of today's mammals, birds and reptiles. Before the amphibians crawled onto land, it was covered by mosses and other simple plants which developed 450 million years ago.

Fungi and insects

The amphibians fed on these mosses and other plants. They slowly developed and more diverse organisms came into being. Fungi also evolved and they too fed on mosses. The earliest land animals are said to be tiny creatures the size of woodlice. Along this time, creatures such as spiders, dragonflies and other insects evolved, which exist even today.

The first four-legged animal came into existed more than 350 million years ago. Then came the dinosaurs about 130 million years ago. The first human beings (called hominid) came into existence only 4 million years ago.

ECOSYSTEMS AND FOOD CHAINS

The biosphere is called the "global ecosystem". It is made up of living organisms such as plants and animals. These are biotic components or biota. It is also composed of non-living organisms such as a lake, soil and precipitation. These are abiotic components.

An ecosystem

An ecosystem is a community of living organisms, in an area, interacting with each other and also with the abiotic components. The biotic and abiotic components are linked together by energy flows and nutrient cycles. So, not just Earth but parts within Earth can also be called "ecosystem". A single tree can be called an ecosystem as biotic components depend on it for food and it requires energy from abiotic components to survive. The forest in which it lies can also be called an ecosystem.

Primary producers

All living organisms directly or indirectly depend upon green plants. They are just as important for the survival of life as water. Plants require sunlight to carry out the process of photosynthesis. They produce food and spread it to different parts of the plant. They also give out oxygen, which is required by all living animals for respiration. Animals take in these nutrients when they eat these plants. This is why plants are called "primary producers" or "autotrophs".

Primary and secondary consumers

Those animals that eat plants or depend upon them for food are called "primary consumers" or "herbivores". A cow is a herbivore as it eats grass. Animals that eat herbivores are called "secondary consumers". Most secondary consumers are called "carnivores" as they eat the flesh of other animals. A toad is a secondary consumer as it eats grasshoppers, which are herbivores.

Tertiary and quaternary consumers

Tertiary consumers are larger animals. They only feed upon secondary consumers. An example of this is an owl who eats snakes. Tertiary consumers are eaten by quaternary consumers. A hawk feeds upon an owl, so it is a quaternary consumer. The quaternary consumer is considered "top predator" in a food chain as it does not have natural enemies. Hence, the hawk is a top consumer in its food chain.

Food chain

A food chain is the sequence in which living organisms feed on each other. There is a food chain present in all ecosystems. As we have read so far, producers and consumers together make up the food chain.

All animals, once they die, decompose and give nutrients to the soil, which are useful to produce primary producers. Without any one of these producers and consumers, an ecosystem would be in grave danger.

Secondary Consumer.

Primary Consumer.

Decomposed Animal.

Adapting and Evolving

It is said that Earth is home to more than 10 to 30 million species of life. Of these, only 2 million have been discovered, named and studied. This huge diversity experienced on Earth is said to be the result of "evolution".

What is evolution?

All of the living things we see today are said to have evolved from their predecessors. This evolution is a result of minor or major changes that are witnessed in every generation of a species. In simple terms, evolution is described as succession with modification.

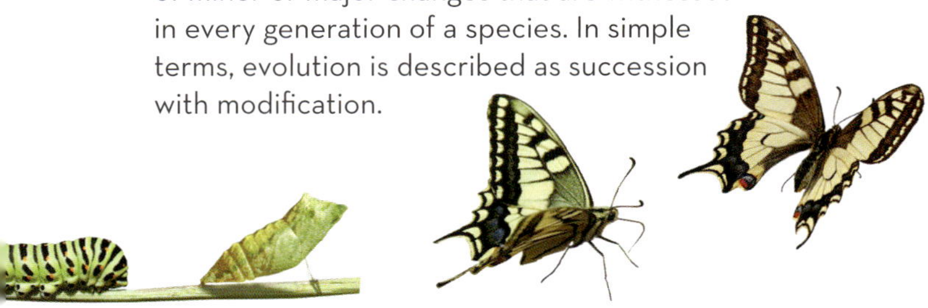

Natural selection

There are variations that take place in a species as it moves towards the next generation. These variations are hereditary. Nature helps develop certain variations based on usefulness to enable a species to survive. "Favourable variations" are those which are useful for simple survival or reproduction. While these are retained or even improved upon with every new generation, the impact of the less favourable variations is diminished or removed entirely. This is called "natural selection". With this, each organism is able to adapt and evolve according to their environment.

Charles Darwin

The theory of evolution was proposed by Charles Darwin, a nineteenth-century scholar. He stated certain factors that bring about the evolution of all living organisms. They can be considered the processes of evolution. Though his theory was accepted by many, it is said to be incomplete as it does not explain why certain organisms have the features that they do.

Genetic drift

Hereditary variation takes place when an organism undergoes spontaneous changes or "mutations". During this phase, the organism trades or upgrades one variation with another more useful one. Hereditary variation can also take place by a process called "sexual recombination", where two organisms mate and produce an offspring who benefits from the best traits of the parent organisms.

The offspring might also have more variations, which might or might not transfer to their offspring. These variations occur in the offspring by chance through a process called "genetic drift".

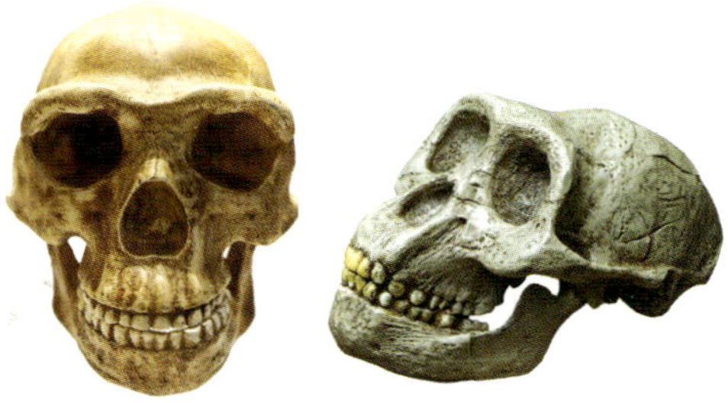

Origins of human beings

Modern human beings belong to a group called "homo sapiens" from the hominini tribe. There is fossilised evidence that proves that homo sapiens have evolved from the predecessors of the hominini tribe. All species of this tribe have shared Earth with ape-like species such as the monkey and the chimpanzee.

Did human beings really descend from apes?

No. This is a popular myth. Human beings are related to apes, but did not descend from them. Animals like the chimpanzee, orangutan and gorilla are direct descendants of the ape family. Apes and human beings have a common ancestor named "Nakalipithecus nakayamai", who is believed to have existed in Africa nearly 11 million years ago. This common ancestor possessed features similar to humans and apes. The hominids and great apes are two of its distinct descendants. They are from two separate branches of evolution.

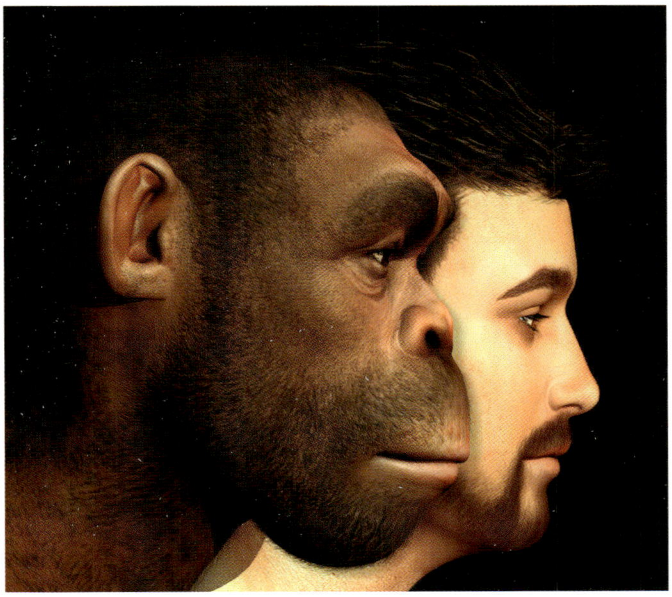

Opposable thumb

Human beings and other primates are "hand-to-mouth" feeders who hold food with the hand and eat it with the mouth. However, one major difference between humans and most primates is the opposable thumb, which means that our thumb can touch all the other fingers of the same hand.

With this thumb, human beings learned to grasp things in their fist; for example, the handle of an axe or the long stick of a spear. While most primates do not have an opposable thumb, some have feet that can grasp onto the branches of trees, an ability that is absent in humans.

FUN FACT

It is believed that the hominini was born in Africa. He then moved to other parts and evolved different physical characteristics as a result of the climate and availability of food.

EXPLORING NEW OPPORTUNITIES

People are always in search of a better life. "Migration" refers to movement from one place to another. Its study can be traced back to the time when the first groups of humans migrated from Africa to other parts of the world. "Human migration" specifically deals with the reasons behind why a group or individual might want to permanently change their location.

Internal and international migration

Migration can be of two types—internal and international. Internal migration is when people move within the same country. For example, a person can move from a village to a city, or from one city to another. International migration is when a person moves from one country to another. For example, a person can decide to move from Mumbai, India, to Paris, France. A person who leaves their country to move to another is called an "emigrant", while a person who has moved to another country is called an immigrant.

A large group of people might migrate to another country together during crisis times like war or an epidemic.

Voluntary and involuntary migration

When people willingly migrate to another location in search of better living conditions or opportunities, it is called "voluntary migration". Not all migrations are voluntary. Some people are either forced or have to flee their location due to bad conditions such as famine or natural disasters.

Some might choose to flee from their countries because of war. These people do not leave with many possessions. They flee without knowing where to go or settle. They do not have an idea of where their new home might be. These people are called "refugees".

Push factors

If a country experiences a lot of crime or war, people of that country might feel unsafe and choose to flee. Farmers would not want to reside in an area that experiences too many floods, droughts or crop failures. People also tend to leave places that do not provide basic services or experience poverty.

Push and pull

People might choose to migrate due to certain opportunities they see in other countries or certain deficiencies in their own. These factors are called "push and pull factors". People tend to migrate due a combination of these factors.

A sudden natural disaster can cause great loss to life and property. It forces the people of the area to move temporarily or permanently.

There was a lot of migration during World War I and World War II.

Pull factors

A country or city which has more opportunities of employment, higher wages and offers more services tends to attract migrants. Farmers like to migrate to places that experience stable weather, fertile lands and a lower risk of natural disasters. Countries that have political and economic stability are also more attractive to migrants.

Farmers during a harvest.

FUN FACT

During the partition of India and Pakistan, nearly 14 million people migrated to go to either India or Pakistan.

Slave migrations

Slave migrations were legally carried out during the sixteenth and nineteenth centuries. The imperialistic European nations, operating from the continents of Africa and Asia, consigned nearly 20 million slaves to their colonies in the Americas through the Atlantic passage.

Slave migration was a practice of the colonial era.

Mass expulsions

Mass expulsion is a form of deportation, which is done by the official channels by government instruction. They are carried out when the official bodies of a country believe that the presence of a certain group of people is illegal or damaging to the country.

In human history, large-scale mass expulsions were carried out during World War I and World War II. During World War II, Nazi Germany had deported close to 8 million people from Germany. The Soviet Union had deported some 11 million people of German descent or nationalities back to Germany.

Effect of the industrial era

Economic conditions have forever been the main reason behind human migration. This trend started from the twentieth century where people moved from the rural and agricultural villages to the industrial cities. Even today, people move from developing continents to developed continents in search of jobs and opportunities to raise their standard of living.

CITIES OF THE WORLD

Nearly 8,000 years ago, the human population lived in rural villages and towns. Cities only came about in the nineteenth century as a direct result of the industrial revolution. They are highly organised and more developed than towns and villages.

Barcelona, Spain

Barcelona is one of the most congested yet beautiful cities in the world. A seaport, it is located by the Mediterranean Sea. In fact, due to its strategic location, until the nineteenth century, this city was very heavily fortified. It was a port of importance for European powers. The work done by distinguished architects over time has given Barcelona a reputation for having one of the most stylish and original skylines in the world.

The Barcelona skyline.

FUN FACT

A skyline is the outline of the mountains, buildings and other high structures of a city against the background of the sky. It is very unique as no two cities have the same skyline.

Athens, Greece

Athens is the national capital city of Greece. It was historically known as a centre for creativity, originality and intellect. It is also considered to be the birthplace of the western civilisation. Athens is the first European city you will see if you are entering from the Middle East. Its food, music, culture and dance is deeply influenced by the East. This city has rebuilt itself several times after almost being destroyed by the devastation of war.

The Parthenon temple is an important monument in Athenian and Greek history.

Paris, France

Paris, the capital city of France, has always been considered as one of the most attractive places in the world. Not only is it an important economic centre in Europe, but it is also known for its food, entertainment, culture, art and literature. It was called the "City of Light", during the Enlightenment. It is also referred to as the "City of Love".

Paris still gives great importance to the education and intellectual growth of its population. The Eiffel Tower is one of its main attractions, followed by the Louvre, the most popular museum in the world.

A view of Paris with the Eiffel Tower in the distance.

Shoreline view of the city of Istanbul, Turkey.

Istanbul, Turkey

The capital city of Turkey, Istanbul is known for its rich culture that is reflected in the architecture of the city. The old city continues to show glimpses of the famous empires that once ruled this city and gave it its glorious history. Istanbul is one of the most populated city in Turkey, while also serving as its economic and cultural capital. This city also stretches across both Europe and Asia, making it a transcontinental city.

Passing through the Grand Canal in Venice from a gondola is a major attraction.

Venice, Italy

Venice, an island city, is a major seaport of Italy. It has a wonderfully unique layout with more than 200 canals making up its transport network. Its narrow streets do not allow for extensive travel by automobiles. Most of its people commute via boats and ferries. The most popular form of transport for tourists is the gondola. This city is considered an artistic and architectural treat for all travellers.

A lighthouse on a beach in Colombo.

Colombo, Sri Lanka

Colombo, the national capital of Sri Lanka, is the principal port of the Indian Ocean. It is known for its artificial harbour, which is one of the largest in the world. The Colombian port was mentioned back in the fifth century in Chinese traveller Faxian's accounts. Historically, it has attracted many foreign travellers like the Arabs, British and Portuguese, and has always been a place of financial and political importance.

Jakarta, Indonesia is the second largest megacity after Tokyo.

Megacities

"Megacities" is the name given to those cities who have a population of more than 10 million people. Most developing countries, such as India and Pakistan, have megacities because of the large number of people who migrate from rural areas to urban areas. Additionally, developing countries have fewer cities for people to choose from.

Tokyo, Japan, is the world's largest megacity with a population of more than 36 million people. Jakarta, Indonesia and Seoul, South Korea are the second and third largest megacities in the world.

The bustling and busy city of Tokyo.

POPULATION DISTRIBUTION

Starting from the 2000s, more and more people around the world migrated to cities from rural areas. By the year 2030, it is believed that about 60 per cent of the world population will be living in cities. Cities are continuing to grow as more and more people shift to urban areas.

What is population distribution?

The term "population distribution" describes where people of the world live and how they are spread across the world. It takes into account which places are lived in by people and why those people have chosen to live there. This study of population is made to understand human behaviour and preferences.

Population density

This is a number calculated to help understand population distribution. It takes into account how many people live in 1 square km or 1 square mile. It is from this data that we know the total population of a place. It is surprising then to know that there are more "empty areas" (where humans do not live) in the world than "occupied areas". A large part of the world population is concentrated in developing countries like India.

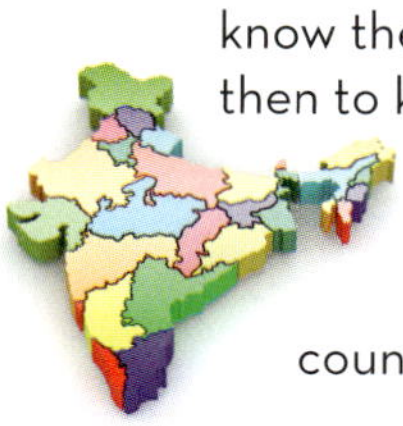

Physical factors

People choose where to live based on certain physical factors. Antarctica has a permanent zero population because of its harsh climatic conditions. Lack of fresh drinking water, extreme temperatures, low vegetation and low availability of food are some physical factors which discourage people from living in a place.

On the other hand, places with fertile soils, plenty of available natural resources, pleasant climate and plenty of food encourage people to settle there.

Why do some places have low population?

People flock to places with more employment opportunities as it allows them to earn money. They prefer places that offer good services like education, healthcare, entertainment and recreation. Hence, a place which does not provide enough of these services and requirements remains thinly populated. The people living in such places might choose to move away to seek more employment, entertainment or education opportunities.

UNICELLULAR AND MULTICELLULAR ORGANISMS

The word "biodiversity" is a combination of the two words—biological and diversity. It is used to describe the different species and types of life that exist on Earth. This means that the single-celled algae, animals, plants and trees (aquatic, terrestrial or aerial) living on Earth make up its biodiversity.

Unicellular organisms

While plants and animals are made up of millions of cells, a unicellular organism is made up of only one cell. There are three main types of unicellular organisms which exist in all biomes:

Bacteria: Bacteria have a diameter which can be one-thousandth of a millimetre. They cannot be seen without a microscope. Bacterial cells do not possess a nucleus. However, they might or might not contain a flagellum, which is used for movement. Every bacterial cell has a membrane and cell well as well as the chromosomal DNA.

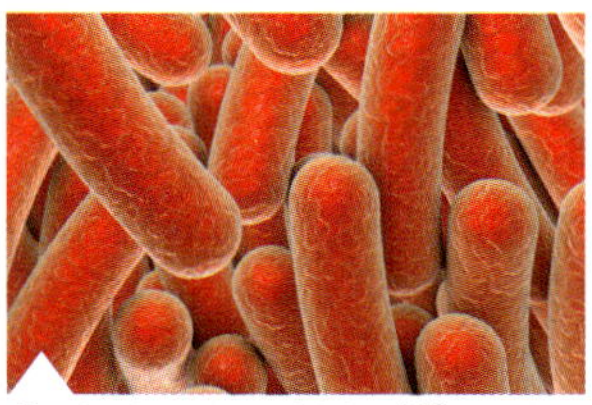

Bacteria can exist in different shapes, sizes and colours.

Protozoa: Protozoa like to live in moist places and largely live in water. They have animal-like features which have developed through adaptations. Protozoa has pseudopodia which takes food into the cell. The contractile vacuoles in the cell allow for waste removal. Protozoa use pseudopodia to move.

Amoeba is an example of a protozoa.

Yeast: This is a type of fungi which is only made up of one cell. Yeast is used to convert sugar into alcohol. They have plant-like cells and cell walls. However, they do not have chloroplasts so they must absorb sugar to gain nutrition.

A microscopic view of yeast cells.

Protista: These are microscopic single-celled organisms. They are made up of eukaryotic cells, unlike bacteria which are made up of prokaryotic cells. Protists are a very large, diverse group of organisms, including the plant-like protists (algae), fungi-like protists, and the animal-like protists (protozoans).

Patterns made on the water surface.

Fungi

Except yeast, fungi (plural of "fungus") are multicellular organisms. Fungi cannot make their own food as they do not contain chloroplasts. They feed on plants and plant-like organisms that make their own food. However, some fungi and algae live together and the algae produces food for the fungi.

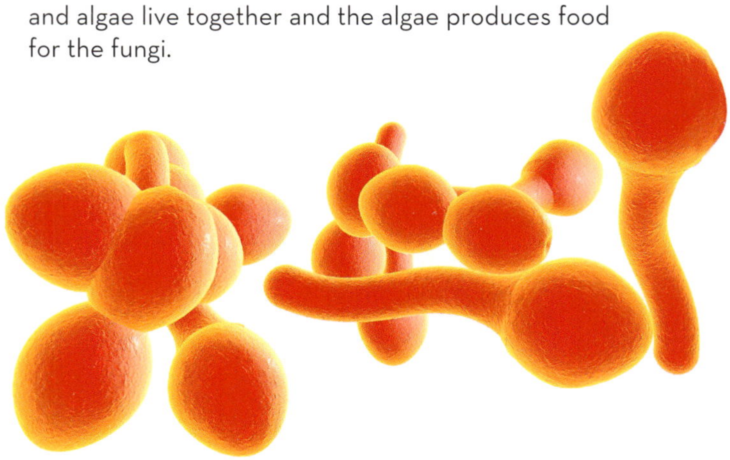

Multicellular organisms

These organisms are made up of many cells which might exist independently or in integrated groups. Here, different cells or groups of cells are assigned different tasks. Some of these are called specialised cells. Many multicellular organisms also form tissues and organs.

INTELLIGENT MAMMALS

Mammals are the most intelligent animals. They are animals with hair or fur covering their bodies. The females carry their young ones in their wombs and then give birth to them. The young ones feed on their mother's milk. Additionally, all mammals are vertebrates, which means that they have backbones. Human beings are mammals because they meet these conditions.

Mammal babies

Some mammal babies are very weak when they are born. Some are born with their eyes firmly shut. Some are born without the ability to walk. They must learn to do these things as they grow.

As babies, all mammals feed on their mother's milk. All female mammals have mammary glands which produce milk. Only mammals can produce their own milk. As they grow up, mammal babies learn to eat the food their parents eat

The young ones

Most mammal babies must stick to their mothers (or fathers) after birth as they are unable to do things by themselves. A kangaroo baby (called "joey") is as small as the thumb when born. It must live in its mama's pouch which is near its stomach. After a few weeks, it peeks outside the pouch. Some weeks later, it comes outside for a little time, then rushes back into the pouch when it is scared or tired. At ten months old, it is ready to hop besides its mother.

The koala baby rides its mother's back as she goes hunting for food. The koala mother hunts for food on treetops and the koala baby hangs on tight. Once they grow up, they feel strong and confident enough to leave their mama's and go hunting and feeding on their own.

Eating habits

Once mammal babies develop their teeth, they begin to eat solid foods like grass, leaves or meat. The papa wolf hunts for meat, chews it up then spits it out for his babies. The baby wolves first play with the meat and then taste it. They like it and begin to eat meat. They don't go back to milk again. This is the same for lions and tigers.

A cub learning to eat meat.

A time for learning

Baby mammals learn to walk, eat, hunt and play from their parents. As babies, they observe their parents and other adult animals and pick up their habits. When the mama bear eats berries and catches fishes, the baby bear watches her and then slowly tries it herself. If the baby elephant tries to leave its mother, she will push it with her big trunk. This teaches the baby elephant to stay with its herd.

A mother kangaroo with its joey in its pouch.

COLD-BLOODED REPTILES

Reptiles are animals whose bodies covered with scales. The young ones hatch from eggs. A reptile is a cold-blooded animal, which means it cannot regulate its own body temperature. This is different from warm-blooded animals, like mammals, whose body temperatures remain the same.

Laying eggs

Turtles, snakes, lizards, alligators and crocodiles are reptiles. All reptiles lay eggs. An alligator lays its eggs and stays close to them for two months until the eggs hatch. Once they do, it leaves. Turtles dig holes in the ground and lay their eggs in the holes. They cover them up with twigs, sticks and mud so that they are hidden. Then, they leave.

Eggs are hatched under the heat of the Sun. Baby turtles climb out of the hole in search of food. Parent reptiles do not help their young ones grow up. Some kinds of snakes warm and protect their eggs by rolling their bodies around them. Once they hatch, the snakes leave.

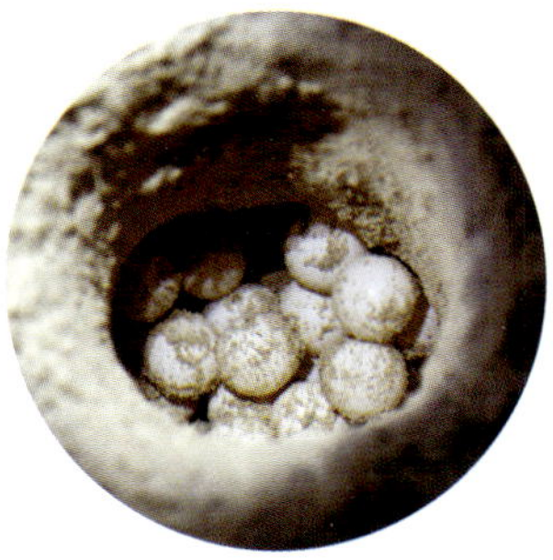

It becomes difficult for predators to find the eggs of turtles.

Shedding skin

Reptiles like snakes and lizards shed their skin. As snakes grow, they become too big for their skin. They grow new skin underneath. The old skin becomes loose and wrinkly. As they move, the skin begins to peel off.

Snake skin hanging from a branch.

Snakes rub their mouth against rough surfaces so that the old skin cracks. Then, as they crawl between smooth rocks and hard branches, the skin begins to crackle and break. The old skin then hangs on the tip of the tail until the snake rubs it between some branches and trees. The skin falls away, leaving the snake with its shiny new skin.

Shedding skin and losing tails

Lizards have legs, so they cannot crawl against surfaces and have their old skin break off. They tear their old skin off with their mouth. Some even feed on their old skin. Snakes and lizards do not feel pain when they shed their skin. If a lizard's tail breaks off, it simply grows a new one. It does not feel pain upon losing its tail.

Flexible mouths

Snakes feed on rats, lizards and rabbits. They also eat eggs and, sometimes, even eat other snakes. Snakes tend to swallow their food whole. They can open their mouths very wide in order to accommodate the size of their food. Then, the juices in their mouth allow the food to pass through. The bones in their throats cut and crack their food, and they spit out the remnants.

ADAPTIVE AMPHIBIANS

Animals that can live on land and water are called "amphibians". All amphibians are vertebrates, which means that they have a backbone. Historically, it is believed that the first vertebrates on Earth were amphibians. Amphibians are also considered to be the ancestors of mammals and reptiles. Toads, frogs and salamanders are amphibians.

Life cycle

The female amphibian lays its eggs in water. Then, it leaves. The eggs might survive in the water as larva, which slowly matures. The stage after this is called the "tadpole" stage where the baby frog or toad emerges from the egg with a tail. At this stage, amphibians have gills, which allow them to breathe underwater.

As they grow into adults, the larva loses its gills and develops lungs. Some amphibians lose their tails and develop front and back legs. Now, amphibians are able to live on land for part of their lives. This development is called "metamorphosis" because the young amphibian changes beyond recognition.

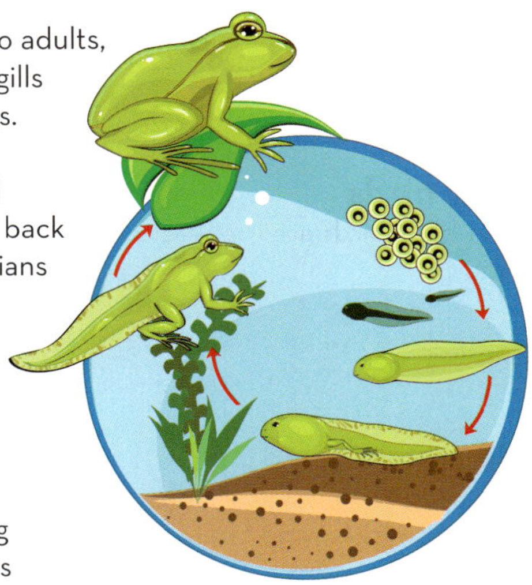

Life cycle of a frog.

Salamanders

Salamanders and newts have tails. Depending on the species, they vary in size. While some can be tinier than your thumb, others can be larger than an adult human. Salamanders also have thin bodies with four legs. Like reptiles, a salamander is able to grow back its tail and even its legs if it loses them.

Caecilians

The appearance of Caecilians bears a resemblance to that of worms. The larger ones in this group look more like snakes. Like worms or snakes, caecilians do not have arms or legs; they are limbless. They have thin, elongated bodies. Their skin covers their eyes, which indicates that these animals are partially or completely blind. Caecilians like to remain hidden underground or live in water.

Caecilians look like big worms.

Toads and frogs

At first glance, you might not be able to differentiate between a frog and a toad. They have various overlapping characteristics; they have a similar body structure and no tail. Both have eyes on top of their heads. However, a toad is bigger and fatter. Its back legs are smaller and shorter. Its skin has warts and is rough and bumpy to touch. A frog's skin is smooth and shiny. It feels wet to touch.

Toad's skin is rough and bumpy to touch.

FEATHERY BIRDS

A bird is a bipedal, warm-blooded animal, a vertebrate, covered in feathers and lays eggs. Bipedal: All birds have two legs used for perching, walking, hopping or running. Birds are warm-blooded animals. Their bodies are covered with feathers that act as insulation. They lay eggs. Birds are bipedal or have two legs that are used for perching, walking and hopping .

Features

Birds are warm-blooded vertebrates. Instead of forelimbs, birds have wings which enable them to fly. All birds have sharp vision which provides them with information about their surroundings. However, their sense of smell and hearing is not as sharp.

Birds have beaks instead of mouths.

Feathers

Birds are said to descend from reptiles. Their scales were evolved into feathers. There are different types of feathers on a bird's body. Unlike hair or fur, feathers only cover some part of a bird's body. Usually, the area near the leg is simply exposed skin. Soft feathers cover the inner portion of the bird's body. These feathers are called down feathers. The down feathers keep the bird warm. The others are used to fly.

The peacock is the male bird of this species. It has long, beautiful feathers. The peahen has brown, plain feathers.

Coming out of the egg

Birds lay eggs in order to reproduce. The baby bird slowly develops in the egg. The egg has all the food it might need already present inside. The head of the baby bird is bigger than its body and its eyes are tightly shut. When it is ready, the baby bird uses the tiny tooth on its bill to crack open the egg and push its way out. It loses this tooth a few days later as it no longer needs it.

Baby birds

Most baby birds are too weak. They stay in the nest or close to it with their eyes tightly shut. At this stage, their bodies do not have feathers and their legs are too weak for them to stand for too long. During this time, the mother bird hunts for food like little worms and feeds it to her babies.

However, some birds like baby flamingos, ducks, chickens and geese have wide open eyes and they are able to leave their nest a few minutes after they hatch from the eggs. They follow their mother around in the hopes that she will give them food.

Baby ducks imprint on their mothers so that they do not lose her. Then they follow her around, no matter where she goes, to get food.

FINNY FISH

What is a fish? A fish is an aquatic animal that lives in water. However, not all animals that live in water can be called fish. Dolphins and whales are mammals, not fish. The body of a fish is covered with scales. A fish swims with the help of fins and a tail, and has gills to breathe.

Fins and eyes

Fish have big eyes which always seem to be left open. This is because they do not have any eyelids. Some fish cannot see. Due to this, they have a developed sense of smell, which helps them understand their environment. Fish swim with the help of their fins. They steer themselves in the water with the help of their fins. They have one big fin on their back, two smaller ones on their sides, and a broad fin called a tail.

All fish more or less have the same number of fins in the same position.

Gills

Fish have small slits at the front of their heads. They are placed right behind or next to the mouth. They are gills. Fish take in the oxygen mixed with the water through their gills. They let out carbon dioxide. Aquatic plants use this carbon dioxide to carry out the process of photosynthesis.

Sticky eggs

Fish lay many eggs at one time. Some fish lay thousands of eggs while some lay millions of eggs. This is because fish eggs are very delicate. Unlike bird or reptile eggs, they do not have hard shells. They are soft and jelly-like. They stick to the ocean floor or a rock. Other fish might eat these eggs. Some eggs might float to the top and dry up. Only a handful of the eggs finally give baby fish.

The shiny, sticky eggs of a clownfish have settled on a surface.

Father fish

Father fish aggressively protect and care for their eggs and babies. Some mother fish lay their eggs in the mouths of the father fish. Once the eggs hatch, the father fish spit the babies out. The mother seahorse lays her eggs in the pouch of the father seahorse. Baby seahorses come shooting out of this pouch when they are ready. Most father fish guard the nests or spots where the eggs are laid. They fight anything that comes near, sometimes even the mother fish. Once they hatch, father fish teach their babies to swim and feed them food.

MANY-LEGGED ARTHROPODS

Arthropods belong to a class of animals called "Arthropoda". They are classified into insects, arachnids and crustaceans based on how many legs they have. Insects have six legs, arachnids have eight legs and crustaceans have ten legs. There are about a million species of arthropods and billions of each species present on Earth. No matter where you go, you will come across an arthropod.

Six-legged insects

Insects are also called "hexapods" where "hex" means six and "pods" means feet. We can easily differentiate an insect from other types or arthropods by looking at their bodies. An insect has antennae on its head, its eyes and mouth are also present here. The thorax (the part between the head and midsection) of an insect has its six legs and, in the case of adults, its wings. The thorax has three segments. The abdomen has many segments and it contains the organs of reproduction, digestion and excretion.

Insects have antennae on their heads.

Special parts of insects

Insects taste with their feet. One eye of an insect has hundreds of smaller eyes. These eyes capture only part of the image they wish to see. Insects smell with their antennae or "feelers".

Eight-legged arachnids

Spiders are classic examples of arachnids. Mites, daddy longlegs, scorpions and tarantulas are other examples or arachnids. The common feature amongst all of them is that they have eight legs. While some have small, round bodies like the mites, others have large, sharp and pointed bodies like the scorpions. Some have hair while some do not. All arachnids have simple eyes, unlike insects. Most arachnids live on land except for some that either live on, or feed on, water. All arachnids are creatures of prey, which means they are parasitic, or completely eat other creatures.

All spiders make webs, which is their home.

Ten-legged crustaceans

Crustaceans are those arthropods which have crusts on their skin. Crabs, shrimps and lobsters fall under the category of crustaceans. Unlike other arthropods, most crustaceans are aquatic in nature. It is difficult to exactly point out which arthropod is a crustacean and which is not. Some shrimps are microscopic in size. Barnacles do not move. They fix themselves to rocks or bottoms of ships. Lobsters have a long and lean structure, whereas crabs are round and small. Along with ten legs, crustaceans also have four feelers. Most have gills to help them breathe. These are the common identifiers.

Crabs have sharp pincers at the ends of their legs.

All arachnids have eight legs.

THE ANIMAL-HUMAN CONNECTION

There are many ways in which animals have helped improve the lives of human beings. Some animals are studied in order to better understand the world and environment. Some animals are used in experiments. Human beings eat certain animals or animal products. They use animals to make work easier. They wear the skin of some animals. On the other hand, they shelter and protect some animals from hunters.

Working with animals

Did you know that animals can go to doctors too? They are called "veterinarians". Pet owners and people from zoos and wildlife sanctuaries call veterinarians when animals become sick.

Zookeepers look after animals in zoos. They make sure they are fed and clean, and perform regular checks for diseases. They ensure that the animals are happy. Rangers and wardens care for animals in forests, natural enclosures and sanctuaries. People record animals or take their pictures to make nature documentaries.

A zookeeper feeding the lemur under her charge.

Studying animals

Zoologists, ecologists and naturalists study animals. They observe animals from remote laboratories or even from their homes. Sometimes, they go to the wild jungles to find and study the animals of their interest. They capture the animals they have to study. Sometimes, they sedate them with an anaesthetic. They mark the animals with bands around their paws or necks and then set them free again. This helps them recognise the animal they are studying in case of long research projects.

Nature documentaries also explore life underwater with special equipment to capture picture and sound.

Things from animals

We get milk, eggs and meat from animals. This milk is also used to make butter or curd. As children grow, they drink cow's milk. Cows and snakes are also used for leather. Wool from sheep is used to make sweaters. Yaks and horses carry heavy loads on their backs. They are also used for transport.

Making life easier

Some animals make life easier. Herding dogs are trained to keep a flock of sheep in line. If a sheep in the flock appears to be in trouble, they quickly go and alert their master. In very cold places, dogs are trained to pull sleds. Guide dogs are trained to help blind people walk without bumping into obstacles.

Dogs and sheep working together.

ENDANGERED AND EXTINCT ANIMALS

Millions of years ago, various species of dinosaurs roamed on Earth. However, we do not see a single dinosaur today. This is because they are extinct. To be extinct means to no longer exist. Today, there are several species of animals under the threat of being extinct. They are said to be endangered. Animals are said to be endangered if their numbers are suddenly dropping or if they are facing a loss of habitat.

Loss of habitat

Loss of habitat occurs due to natural changes in the climate or due to some external influences. Dinosaurs existed around 65 million years ago. They enjoyed a hot and dry climate. Around this time, an asteroid struck Earth. Because of this, a lot of debris settled into the environment, reducing the cover of heat and light on Earth's surface. The climate became cooler, which the dinosaurs were unable to adapt to. Hence, they slowly became endangered and finally extinct.

Archaeologists have dug up the bones of dinosaurs to study them.

Human contribution to habitat loss

Deforestation is the practice of clearing forests to gain ground and raw materials.

While human beings clear forests to make room for housing, industries and to gain raw materials, they are endangering several species. For example, if a species lives on the pine tree, clearing a pine forest could put this species in danger. Some species that live in the Amazon forests are facing extinction because much of it is being cleared to build ranches, houses and for logging.

Lack of genetic variation

Animals also become endangered or extinct due to the lack of genetic variation. If there is a high population of a species, the genetic variation is more. This is why there is so much genetic variation in human beings in terms of hair, skin and eye colour. With genetic variation, species are better able to adapt to the environment. Hence, a lack of this can put a species under threat.

Genetic variation reduces if there is inbreeding. This means that close family members of a species mate to produce the offspring. This causes serious diseases, which threaten the life of the offspring.

Endangered cheetahs

In Asia and Africa, cheetahs are endangered because of inbreeding. During the last ice age, cheetahs began to inbreed. This reduced the amount of genetic variation in the species. They were soon unable to adapt to their surrounding environment for this reason.

It is difficult to breed cheetahs, so the measures to protect them are very few.

PLANTS AND POLLINATION

Plants can be of two types. These are flowering plants and non-flowering plants. Rose plants, apple trees, pine trees and such other plants and trees are examples of flowering plants. They produce flowers and seeds. Non-flowering plants are those which do not produce flowers and seeds. Moss and fern plants are examples of non-flowering plants.

Growing into a plant

Plant cycle begins from seeds or spores. Non-flowering plants have spores on them. Spores a microscopic reproductive cells. Flowering plants give seeds. These seeds sprout into seedlings underground if they receive sufficient nutrients, water and sunlight.

The spores of a fern plant.

The roots of a plant begin to grow from the seedling and spread into the soil. The stem appears above the soil. Leaves and flower buds then grow on the stem. Over time, the flower buds open to show the flower.

The growing stem and leaves of the seedling have emerged from below the ground.

Production of seeds

Flowering plants produce their own seeds. Most flowers carry pollen which is very small, powdery material. It also comes from some types of weed and grasses. Usually, the pollen grains are carried to other flowers by wind. This is called "pollination".

Some insects also help carry out the process of pollination. Honeybees sit on flowers to take the nectar from it. As they do this, the pollen in the flower sticks to their bodies. As they travel, they carry pollen grains with them. When they sit on another flower, they transfer the pollen to it.

Fertilisation

Petals are the most colourful and beautiful part of the flower and even the plant. They attract insects such as honeybees and butterflies to themselves. These insects then carry out the process of pollination for flowers.

After pollination takes place, pollen grains move to the carpel of the new flower. From here, they move to the ovary and fertilise the ovules, which are egg cells. This is what makes seeds. This is called "fertilisation".

Pollen grains are stuck to the legs of the honeybee.

PLANT REPRODUCTION

The reproductive system of a plant can be sexual or asexual. Flowers are a necessary part of sexual reproduction. Thus, by default, all non-flowering plants carry out asexual reproduction. Plants which have sexual reproduction systems also have male and female cells.

Pollination before sexual reproduction

Before a plant can reproduce, it needs to undergo the process of pollination. During this process, pollen grains move from the anther of one flower to the stigma of on other flower. Pollination can take place in flowering plants by wind or insects. What the flowers of a plant look like depends upon how the pollination takes place.

Male and female parts of the flower

Stamens are the male part of the flower. They produce pollen grains. Pollen grains contain two sperm cells. Carpels contain egg cells which fuse with these sperm cells to fertilise the egg and produce the embryo of the seed. This seed can then germinate into a new plant.

Insect-pollinated flowers

Flowers which are pollinated by insects:

- have bright, colourful feathers; they carry a scent and have nectar.
- have sticky and spiky pollen grains, which stick to the bodies of the insects.
- have anthers and stigma inside the flower. When the insects sit on the flower, the anthers brush against it in order to catch the pollen grains. The stigma is what the pollen grains stick to.
- have fewer pollen grains as pollen grains are spread efficiently with very little loss.

Wind-pollinated flowers

Flowers which are pollinated by wind:

- have small, dullish green or brown petals and do not have scent or nectar as they do not need to attract insects.
- have light pollen grains so that they can easily be carried by wind; the texture is smooth so that they do not clump together.
- have their anthers and stigma outside the flower so that pollen grains can be easily caught by other flowers.
- have lots of pollen grains as not all pollen grains carried by wind get attached to other flowers.

Spreading Seeds

Where do forests come from? Do you think all plants and trees on Earth have been planted by someone? Seeds scatter or disperse and spread to different parts of a landform. They might even move to other landforms. They need to find a new spot to grow as they cannot grow near the parent plant. They might not get enough sunlight and water. This process is called "seed dispersal". There are different methods of dispersal.

Wind

Some seeds are very small and light. They have unique structures. They might have wings or fluffy bits. Maple seeds are examples of winged seeds. Dandelions and milkweed seeds are light and fluffy. Such seeds can easily be carried away by the wind. Maple seeds can travel 180 m from their parent plants. Dandelion and milkweed seeds can travel more than 500 km.

The seeds of the dandelion are separated from the flower.

Water

Some plants and trees grow best near water. Coconut trees are a good example of this. The seeds of these trees water to find a new home to grow on. These seeds waterproof, which means they can safely float in water for hours even if water is extremely salty. They are heavy enough to float. The seeds might be hollow or fluffy to enable them to float in water.

The seeds of the lotus plant are also dispersed from water.

Animals

Some seeds are contained in fruits which animals like to eat. After eating the fruit, the animals might spit or excrete these seeds out of their systems. Squirrels like to eat acorn seeds. They like to store them for winter so they hide them underground. Some squirrels might forget where they have hidden the acorn. These acorns might grow into trees.

The squirrel is looking for a place to hide its acorn.

Hitchhiking seeds

Some seeds are sticky while some seeds have hook-like structures. When an animal interacts with the plant, these seeds stick to the hair or fur on the animal's body. They go where the animals go. Later, they might drop from the animal on a suitable part of land and grow.

Burdock seeds with hook-like structures.

INFINITE ENERGY

Life exists and is sustained by the presence of energy. All living organisms require energy from the Sun. Human beings and animals need some energy from the Sun. Plants need energy for various purposes. Besides the Sun, there are other sources of energy.

Renewable energy

The Sun, wind and water are natural resources. We get heat and light energy from the Sun. Energy from the Sun is called "solar energy". Wind and water move with force. This force helps create energy. Energy from moving wind is called "wind energy". Energy from moving water is called "hydropower". Ocean waves also create energy. This is called "ocean energy".

As long as the Sun exists, we will get energy from it. Energy from the Sun, wind and water can be replenished over and over again. This type of energy, which can be repeatedly replenished, is called "renewable energy".

Biomass

Human and animal excretion (such as manure), wood, biological wastes and alcohol fuels are called "biomass". It is made up of biological matter. Biomass can be used to make biofuel or biodiesel. Biodiesel is made from plant oils and can be used in vehicles that run on diesel. As biomass is made up of renewable organic matter, it is a renewable source of energy.

As long as we keep replanting trees, biomass will remain a renewable source of energy.

Technology

Certain technology is needed to generate or catch energy from renewable sources. For example, solar panels capture solar energy. This energy is then used to light houses. A dam is used to create the force from flowing water. This is then used to generate electricity with the help of turbines. Windmills are used to create wind energy.

Wind turbines generate wind currents from moving wind. These currents are converted to other forms of energy. The force of the wind is converted into a rotational force, which is then used to make an electric generator produce electricity.

Solar panels are fixed to the roofs of some houses so that energy from the Sun can be used for various household purposes.

LIMITED ENERGY

Unlike renewable sources of energy, non-renewable sources cannot be replenished. There is either a limited supply of them on our planet, or creating them takes a very long time. If we do not use them wisely, there is a strong possibility of non-renewable sources of energy being used up completely in our lifetime.

Fossil fuels

One of the most important non-renewable energy resources is fossil fuel. There is energy in all forms of life. Animals and plants store energy for later use. Even after death, they have some amount of energy stored in them. Over millions of years, their remains become fossils. We get fuel from these fossils called "fossil fuels".

A fossil of a plant leaf.

Carboniferous period

It takes millions of years to form fossil fuels. Around 300 years are required for this purpose. This period, in which fossil fuel is formed, is called carboniferous period. The name for this period comes from the word "carbon". Fossil fuels cannot form without carbon. Coal, natural gas and petroleum are examples of fossil fuels. We should be careful about how we use them. If depleted, it will take millions of years for it to form again.

Why does it take millions of years for fossil fuels to form?

Dead plant and animal matter are crushed and pushed under the seabed. Sediments of the seabed as well as rocks, are piled on top of this biological matter. This creates a lot of pressure and heat under the seabed. As a result, with time, plant and animal matter gets converted to fossil fuel. Fossil fuels are stored in reservoirs.

Fossils are also preserved by archaeologists for the study of ancient plants and animals.

An oil rig dug in a part of the ocean.

Coal

When coal is burnt, it produces energy. It is the black rock found in mines. Coal also goes through carbonisation. Dead and buried matter undergo this process to become coal. It takes nearly 10 feet of solid plant matter to create a foot of coal.

Peat and anthracite are two types of coal. Peat is ranked as the least valuable type of coal as it undergoes very little carbonisation. However, it is an important fuel. Anthracite undergoes carbonisation for several years. It is found near mountain ranges and other places where the crust has experienced a lot of movement.

Coal is acquired from underground mines and surface mines.

Petroleum

Petroleum is the liquid form of fossil fuel. It is also called "crude oil". Petroleum is found trapped underground. Sometimes, there is so much pressure underground that petroleum comes bubbling to the surface. The dead remains of animals and plants that roamed on Earth millions of years ago, make up petroleum.

In order to get petroleum, we drill underground. This drilling is done on land and also in the ocean. A place that is being drilled for petroleum is called a "drill rig". An excellent drill rig can provide oil for 30 years or more.

Petrol is used to run cars and other vehicles.

FUN FACT

Natural gas is made mostly of methane, therefore it has the smell of spoiled eggs. It is a fossil fuel which is trapped in reservoirs underground. Around trillion m^3 of natural gas can be found underground.

Nuclear energy

Nuclear energy is a form of renewable energy. However, it comes under the non-renewable energy list because the material needed to make nuclear energy is non-renewable or limited. This material is uranium and it is used in a nuclear power plant. A rare type of uranium is used. Its atomic number is U-235. Most uranium is found in rocks, but U-235 is hard to come by.

Nuclear energy is created through a process called "nuclear fission" which splits an atom. The energy stored in the core or nucleus of an atom is utilised here. This energy is used to generate electricity. Though nuclear energy does not create the kind of damage other forms of energy do, it creates a lot of radioactive waste, which can be highly toxic.

A nuclear plant.

ELEMENTS AND MINERALS

All matter on Earth is made up of atoms. If we take matter like a table or a rock and try to break it down to its smallest component, we will get an atom. An atom an element and it is the smallest element of matter. There are many types of elements on Earth. All elements have certain properties or characteristics which they do not share with other elements.

What are minerals?

Minerals are naturally occurring substances that form rocks. Different types of elements are arranged together to form a mineral. Some minerals are formed entirely from one element. These minerals are considered pure substances and have a high marked value. Diamond is a mineral which is the purest form of carbon. Elements are arranged in a crystal structure. Minerals are raw materials which can be made into clothes, stationery items, furniture and other things, depending upon their properties.

Diamonds have an extremely high value and are used making jewellery.

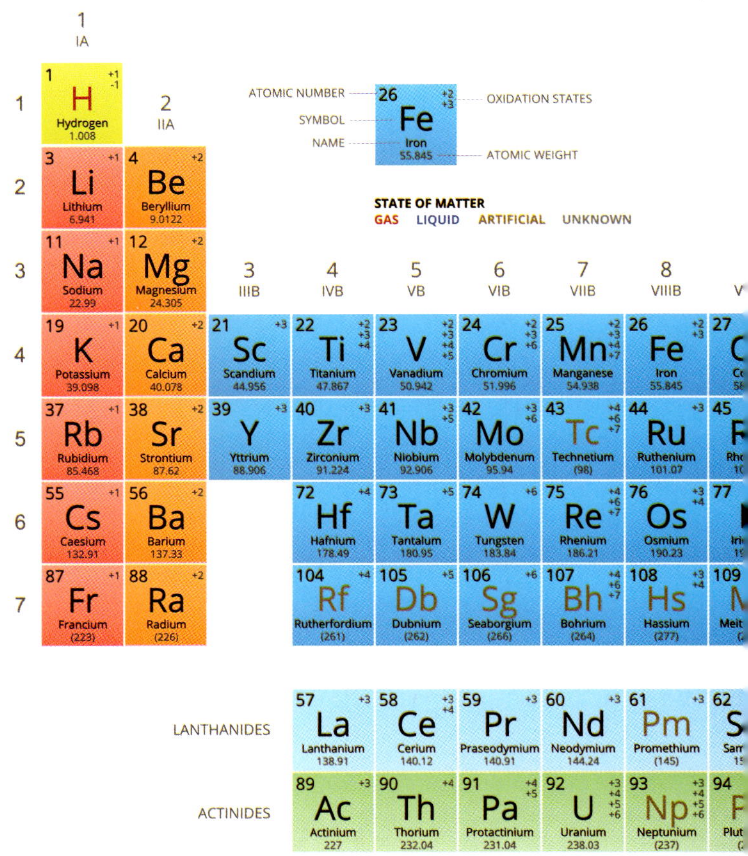

Formation of minerals

Minerals are formed when lava cools to form molten rocks. Magma might cool in underground hollows. Minerals might also form between sediments and other rock structures. Rocks are formed from mineral clusters. Rocks and minerals form certain types of natural resources like granite, marble and iron.

Crystal structure

Imagine that atoms are blocks. To make a structure of these blocks, we must stack them in a structured manner. In the same way, elements are stacked together in a crystal structure. This is a continuous arrangement of elements (whether one or many) to make minerals of different sizes.

The atoms in solids are tightly packed together without any gaps. Because of their structure, most minerals can be cut into crystals that reflect the arrangement of their elements (atoms). These crystals are then polished and cut to form gemstones.

Though the crystal structure of a mineral cannot be seen with the naked eye, we can understand its structure by looking at the mineral.

Halite

Halite is a mineral which is made up of the elements of sodium and chlorine. Its scientific name is sodium chloride. More commonly, it is called rock salt. Sodium and chlorine are stacked together in a cubic shape in the halite mineral. A form of halite is used in cooking. This is not the purest form of halite. Pure halite is actually colourless. It can be tinted in colours by impurities. Geologists identify this mineral by tasting it. Halite deposits are formed by evaporating salt water in oceans and seas.

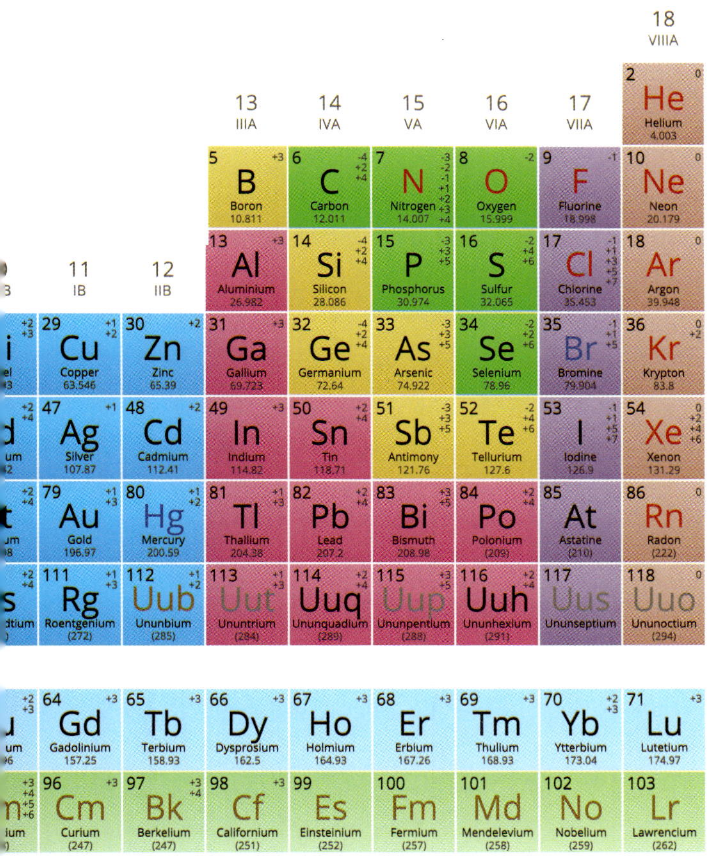

FUN FACT

Talc is the softest mineral on Earth. It is a silicate. This mineral is so soft that we can make scratches on it using our fingernails. Talc feels soapy to touch, which is why it is also popularly known as the soapstone. The talcum powder that we use on our bodies is made from talc.

Mineral classes

There are more than 4,000 naturally occurring minerals on Earth. They are classified into five classes—silicates, carbonates, sulphates, oxides and halides. These classifications are based on the elements and the crystal structure seen in the mineral.

Silicates: In a silicate mineral, one silicone atom is surrounded by four oxygen atoms. They are the largest class of minerals, and also the most complicated of the lot.

Carbonates: Each crystal structure of a carbonate mineral has one carbon atom surrounded by three oxygen atoms. This class of minerals is often found near the surface of Earth's crust.

Sulphates: In a sulphate mineral, one sulphur atom is surrounded by four oxygen atoms. This class has variable properties. Some sulphates are even soluble. Many of them are fluorescent.

Oxides: In oxides, oxygen atoms are stacked with one metal element such as iron. This class includes both hard and soft minerals. While most oxides are black in colour, there are some oxides that are colourful too.

Halides: Halides are types of salts. Their main anions are halogens. Halides are usually soft and transparent.

Calcite and siderite belong to the same mineral class, that is, the carbonate class. In their structure, they both have a carbon atom surrounded by three oxygen atoms. What makes them different is the presence of other elements in their structure. Calcite has the calcium atom in its structure while siderite has an iron atom in its structure.

Quartz is also called silicon dioxide and is the most common silicate mineral.

Calcite is also called calcium carbonate and is found in limestone.

Gypsum is made into a plaster to use in construction.

Hematite an element of iron and is also called iron oxide.

NATURAL TREASURE

Gemstones are the most valuable minerals available on Earth. However, while looking at an uncut gemstone mineral, one might feel that they are very ordinary looking. Gemstones are cut, shaped and polished to form the beautiful, high-value precious stones we see in magazines and jewellery shops.

Precious stones

Gemstones are classified as precious stones and semiprecious stones. Diamonds, rubies and emeralds are precious stones. Diamonds are the hardest minerals and also the hardest naturally occurring substance on Earth. Made entirely of carbon atoms, they look unimpressive in the uncut form. They are formed deep underground because of the high pressure conditions existing here. There are only a few places in the world that have diamonds.

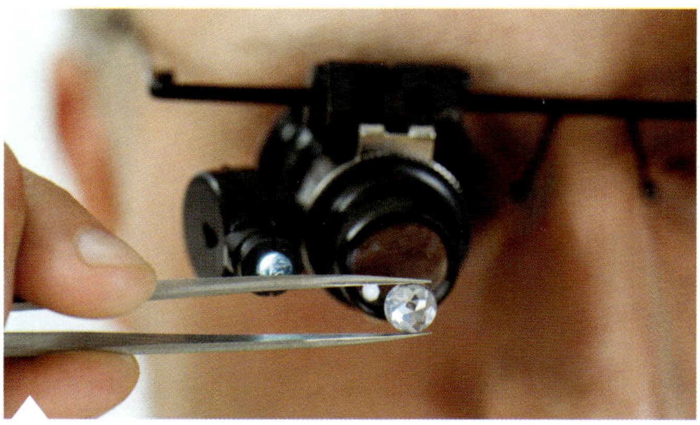

Even a single scratch on a diamond can bring down its value dramatically.

Graphite

Even graphite is a pure carbon mineral. However, the structure of graphite is very different from that of diamond. In the graphite structure, elements are arranged in layers. Because of this difference in structure, graphite is soft and has streaks in its appearance. It is not considered to be a precious stone like the diamond.

Rubies and emeralds

Rubies are formed from aluminium oxide and corundum, which itself is a mineral. Rubies have chromium in small amounts which gives them their red colour. Sapphire is another precious stone formed from corundum. Sapphires come in many colours because of the presence of titanium, chromium or iron.

Emeralds are formed from beryl. Beryl is a mineral with the elements of beryllium, aluminium, silicon and oxygen. It has traces of vanadium and chromium which gives it its colour. Aquamarine is a semiprecious stone formed from traces of other elements mixed with beryl.

The deep red shade of the ruby is very popular and many lipsticks, clothes and shoes have this shade.

Making money with minerals

In ancient times, gold, silver and bronze were used to make currency coins. These metals can be beaten into sheets. They can be made into many shapes. Gold and silver are also used to make articles of jewellery.

Gold

Gold is a very valuable metal. In the past, many people have migrated to areas which have or had gold deposits in the past. They did this in the hopes of discovering gold deposits themselves and to earn a lot of money by selling the deposit. This period of migration was called the "gold rush".